DIGITAL PLANET
HOW DOES SOCIAL MEDIA WORK?

by Nikole Brooks Bethea

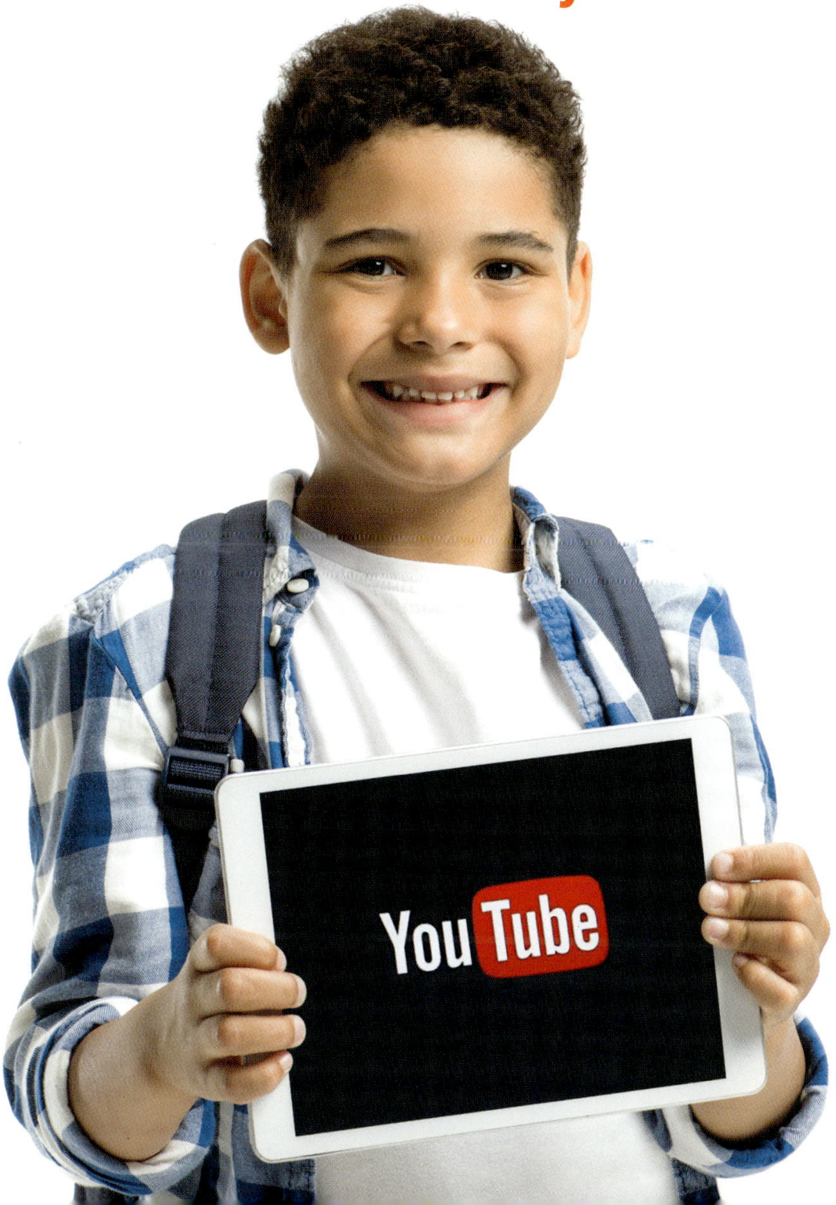

Ideas for Parents and Teachers

Pogo Books let children practice reading informational text while introducing them to nonfiction features such as headings, labels, sidebars, maps, and diagrams, as well as a table of contents, glossary, and index.

Carefully leveled text with a strong photo match offers early fluent readers the support they need to succeed.

Before Reading

- "Walk" through the book and point out the various nonfiction features. Ask the student what purpose each feature serves.
- Look at the glossary together. Read and discuss the words.

Read the Book

- Have the child read the book independently.
- Invite him or her to list questions that arise from reading.

After Reading

- Discuss the child's questions. Talk about how he or she might find answers to those questions.
- Prompt the child to think more. Ask: We use social media to connect with others. Who do you connect with on social media?

Pogo Books are published by Jump!
5357 Penn Avenue South
Minneapolis, MN 55419
www.jumplibrary.com

Copyright © 2020 Jump!
International copyright reserved in all countries. No part of this book may be reproduced in any form without written permission from the publisher.

Library of Congress Cataloging-in-Publication Data

Names: Bethea, Nikole Brooks, author.
Title: How does social media work? / by Nikole Brooks Bethea.
Description: Minneapolis, MN: Jump!, [2020]
Series: Digital planet | Includes index.
Identifiers: LCCN 2019003111 (print)
LCCN 2019005153 (ebook)
ISBN 9781641288927 (ebook)
ISBN 9781641288903 (hardcover: alk. paper)
ISBN 9781641288910 (pbk.)
Subjects: LCSH: Social media—Juvenile literature. | Online social networks—Juvenile literature.
Classification: LCC HM742 (ebook) | LCC HM742 .B48 2020 (print) | DDC 302.23–dc23
LC record available at https://lccn.loc.gov/2019003111

Editor: Susanne Bushman
Designer: Michelle Sonnek
Content Consultant: Sarah McRoberts, Human-Computer Interaction Researcher

Photo Credits: Gcapture/Shutterstock, cover (background); Rawpixel.com/Shutterstock, cover (foreground); LightField Studios/Shutterstock, 1; ArthurStock/Shutterstock, 3; Gregory Johnston/Shutterstock, 4; Andrey_Popov/Shutterstock, 5 (background), 20-21; Monkey Business Images/Shutterstock, 5 (foreground); BigTunaOnline/Shutterstock, 6-7; Alexey Boldin/Shutterstock, 8-9; Veja/Shutterstock, 10-11 (background); Betty LaRue/Alamy, 10-11 (foreground); Vtls/Shutterstock, 12; Susanne Lindholm/AFP/Getty, 13; comzeal images/Shutterstock, 14-15; Evannovostro/Shutterstock, 16-17; Gts/Shutterstock, 18 (background); David MG/Shutterstock, 18 (foreground); Nopanonn/Shutterstock, 19; optimarc/Shutterstock, 23 (background); Natee Meepian/Shutterstock, 23 (foreground).

Printed in the United States of America at Corporate Graphics in North Mankato, Minnesota.

TABLE OF CONTENTS

CHAPTER 1
Connect Online 4

CHAPTER 2
How It Works 12

CHAPTER 3
Be Smart Online 18

ACTIVITIES & TOOLS
Try This! 22
Glossary 23
Index 24
To Learn More 24

CHAPTER 1

CONNECT ONLINE

How do you keep in touch with your friends and family? Do you send mail? Do you talk on the phone?

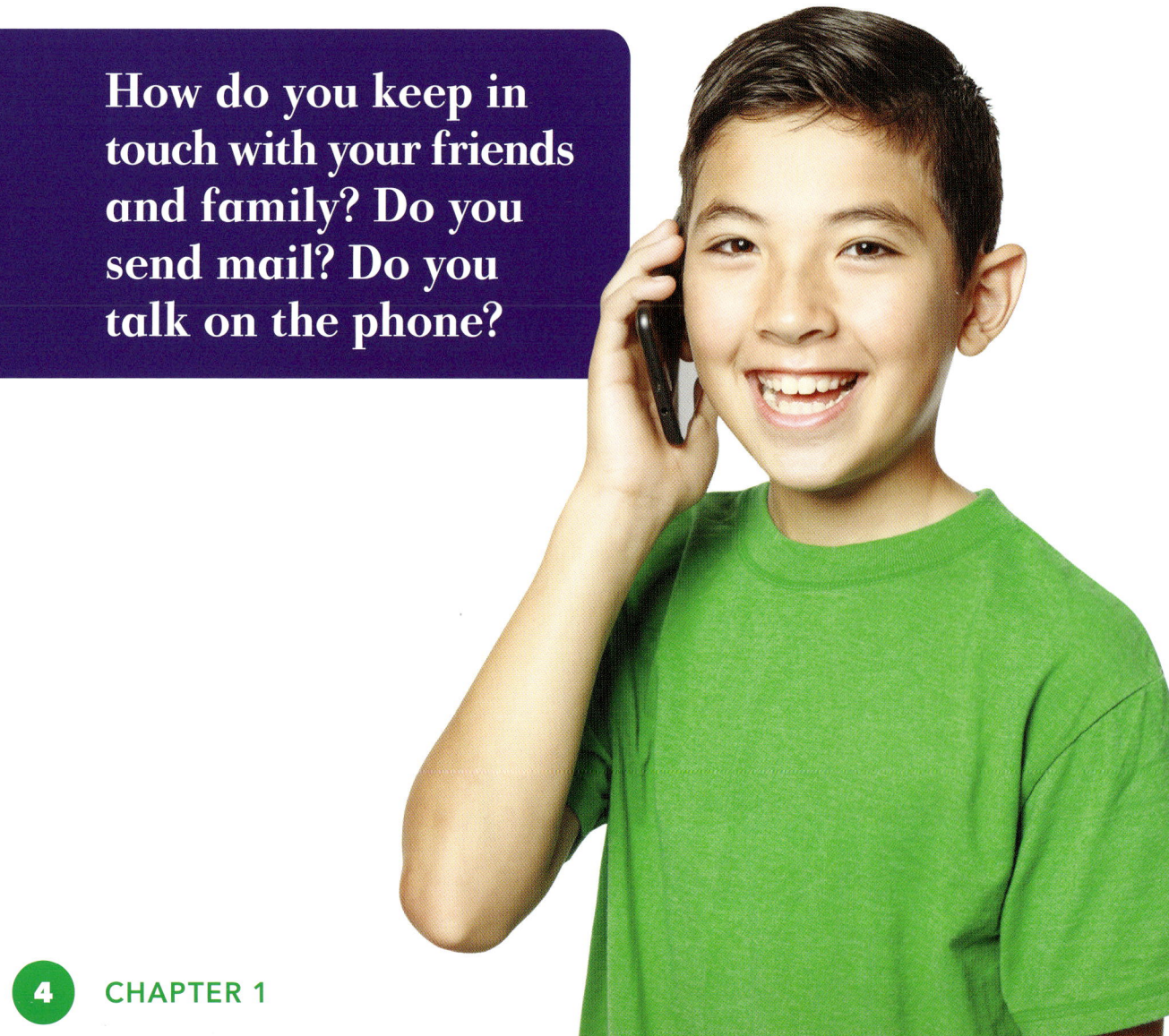

Many of us use social media. These are **interactive** websites. We share our ideas. We **post** about ourselves. We share photos. Our **network** sees them. They can respond. Look! My friend left a comment.

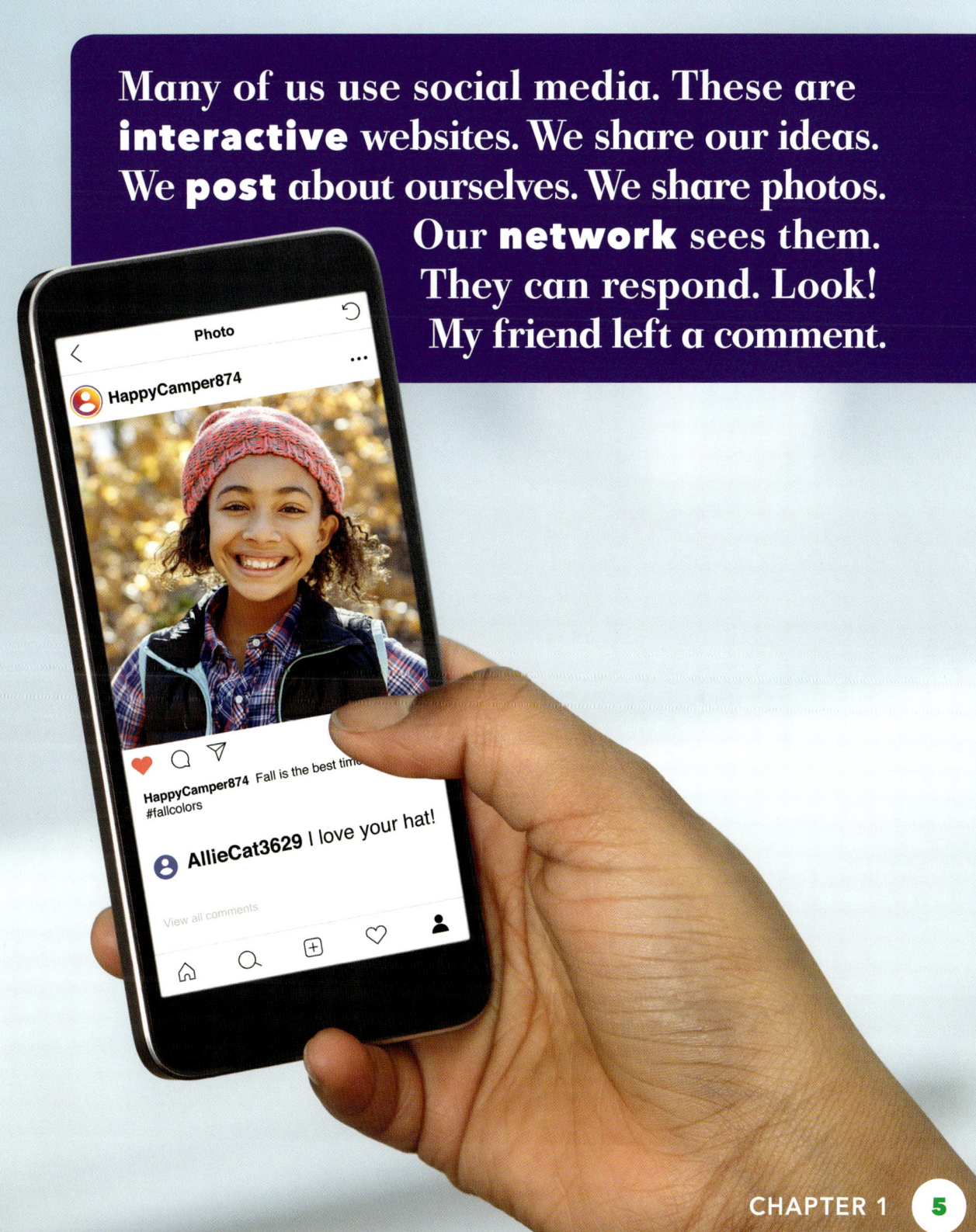

CHAPTER 1   5

We use social media sites and **apps** for different things. We share photos on Instagram. Snapchat sends photos to friends. YouTube users share videos. Twitter users share short posts. They can have images or videos. But they can only use 280 letters or signs!

TAKE A LOOK!

What percentage of U.S. teens used different social media sites in 2018? Take a look!

Site	Percentage
YOUTUBE	85%
INSTAGRAM	72%
SNAPCHAT	69%
FACEBOOK	51%
TWITTER	32%
TUMBLR	9%
REDDIT	7%
NONE OF THE ABOVE	3%

Different sites can have similar features. Like what? A **profile** page is all about a user. It can have your name. Some have photos. They show our interests!

We connect with friends and family. They make up our network. You can see their profiles, too.

We see other users' posts in our **feed**. Posts can be pictures or videos. Some are news or **blogs**. Friends can react to these posts. They can comment, too. Do you comment on others' posts?

Sites let users message. They can talk privately. Some sites have video chat.

DID YOU KNOW?

A **hashtag** is a short phrase. It begins with a #. This links posts. Have you used hashtags?

CHAPTER 2
HOW IT WORKS

Social media sharing creates a lot of **data**! Companies store users' data on **servers**. They link to the internet.

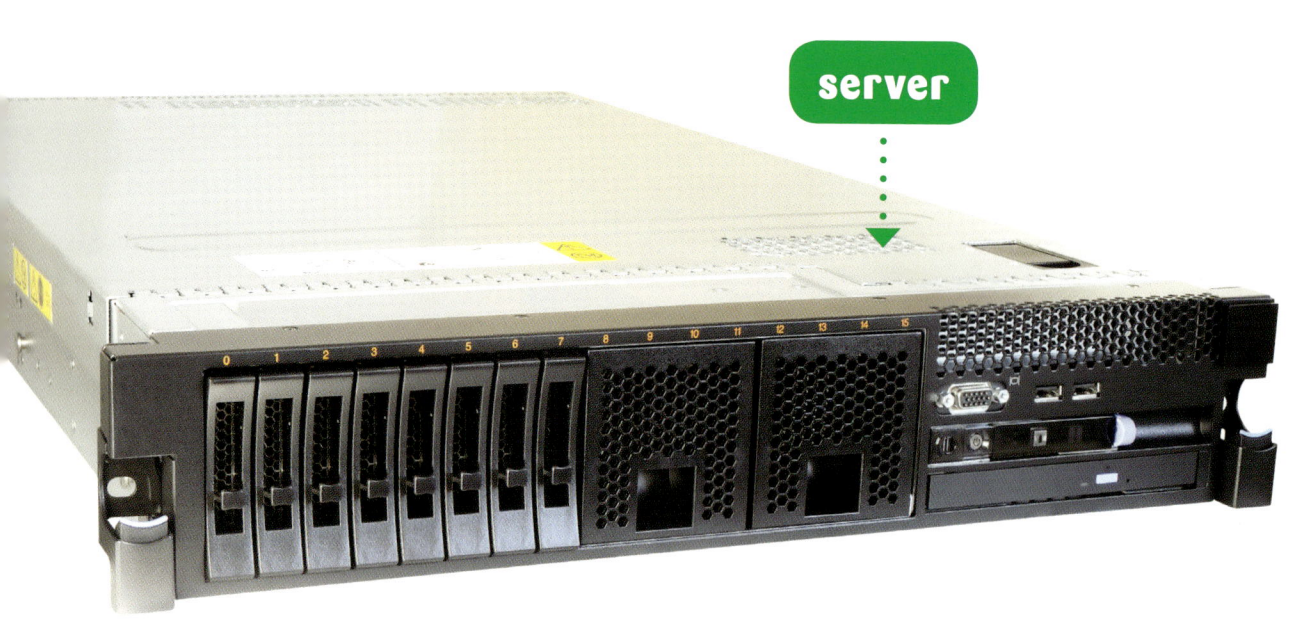

server

Facebook servers

Companies have many servers. Facebook has a server building in Sweden. As of 2019, it was as big as five football fields! Workers get around on scooters.

CHAPTER 2

What happens when you **upload** a picture? Your device links to the internet. The photo file goes to a server.

> ### DID YOU KNOW?
> More than 1 trillion photos are taken each year! About 80 percent are taken on smartphones. Many go on social media!

CHAPTER 2

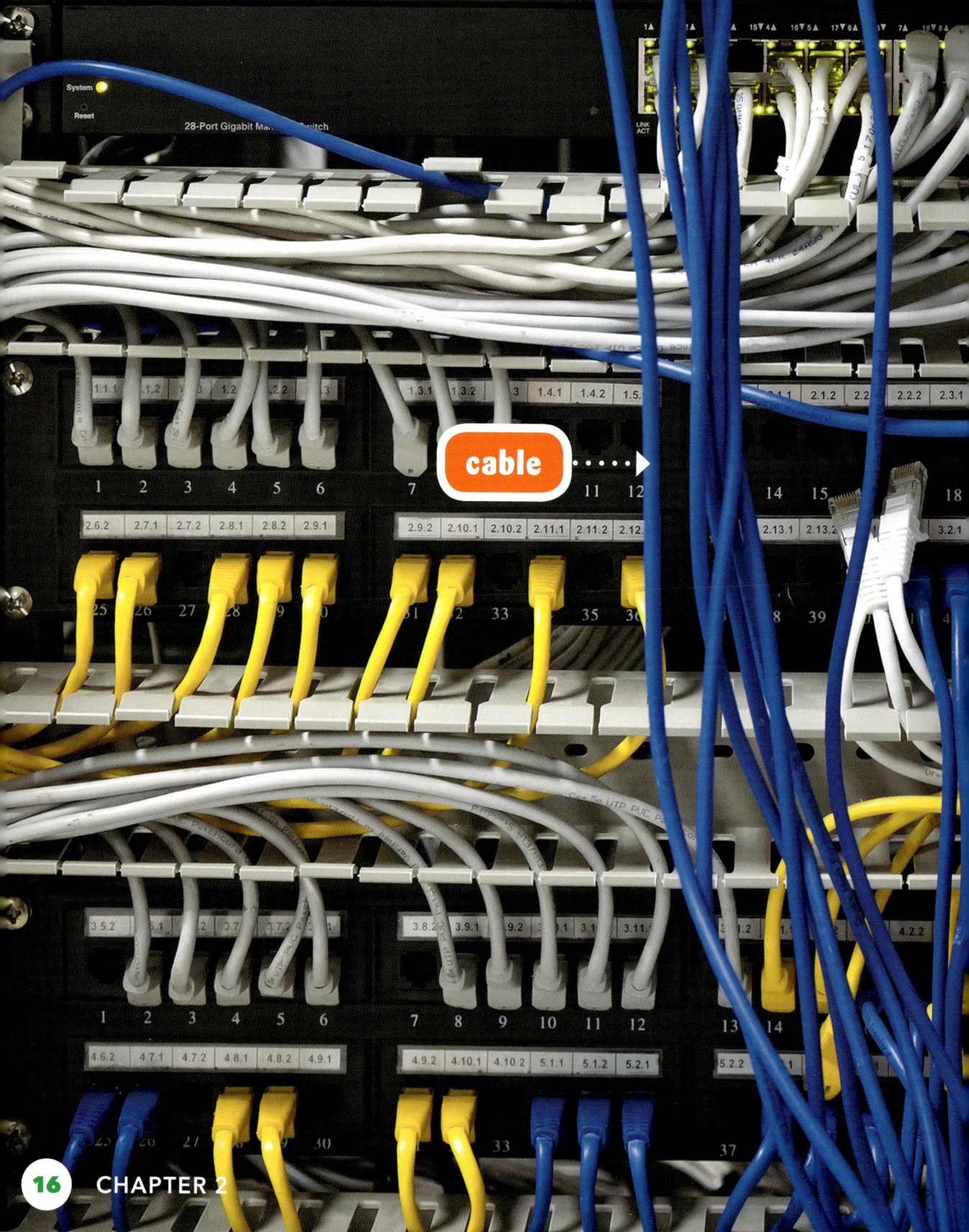

A photo file is big. It cannot send all at once. It breaks into **packets**. Then **routers** guide them. They move through wires called cables. This is how they get to a server. This takes just seconds! Wow!

CHAPTER 2 17

CHAPTER 3
BE SMART ONLINE

Social media is fun. But it can be unsafe. Be careful! Only connect with people you know. Check your privacy settings. Make a strong password.

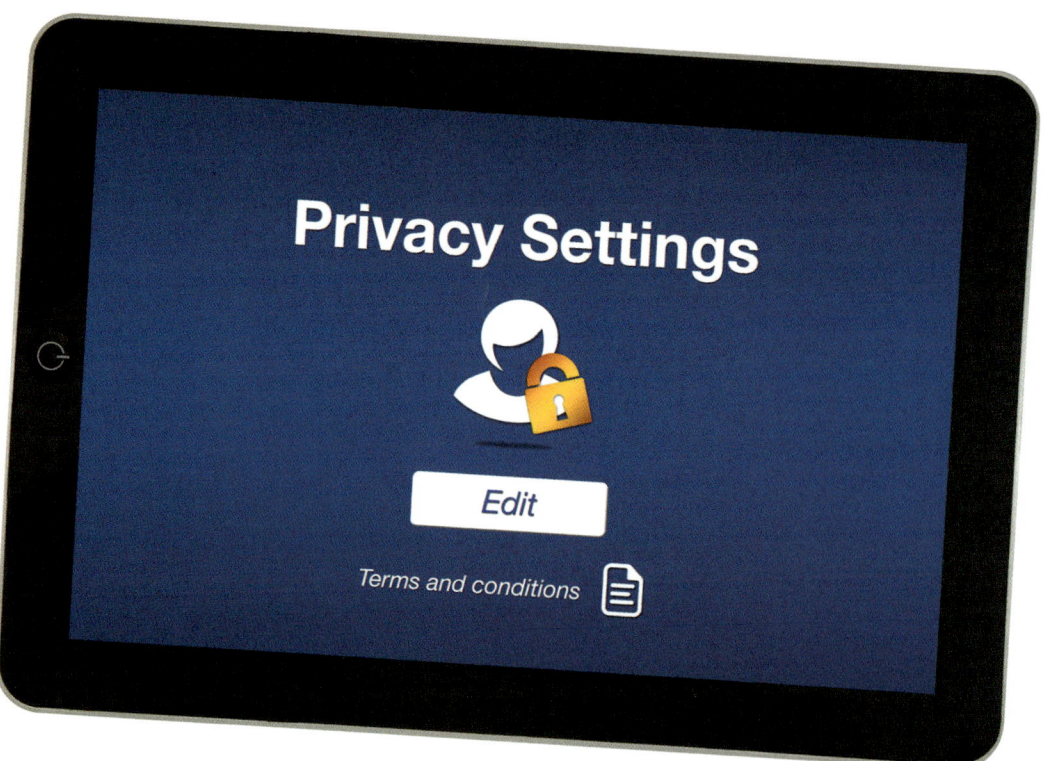

Beware of fake news. This is false information. People can share it on social media. This can make it look and seem real.

fake news

CHAPTER 3

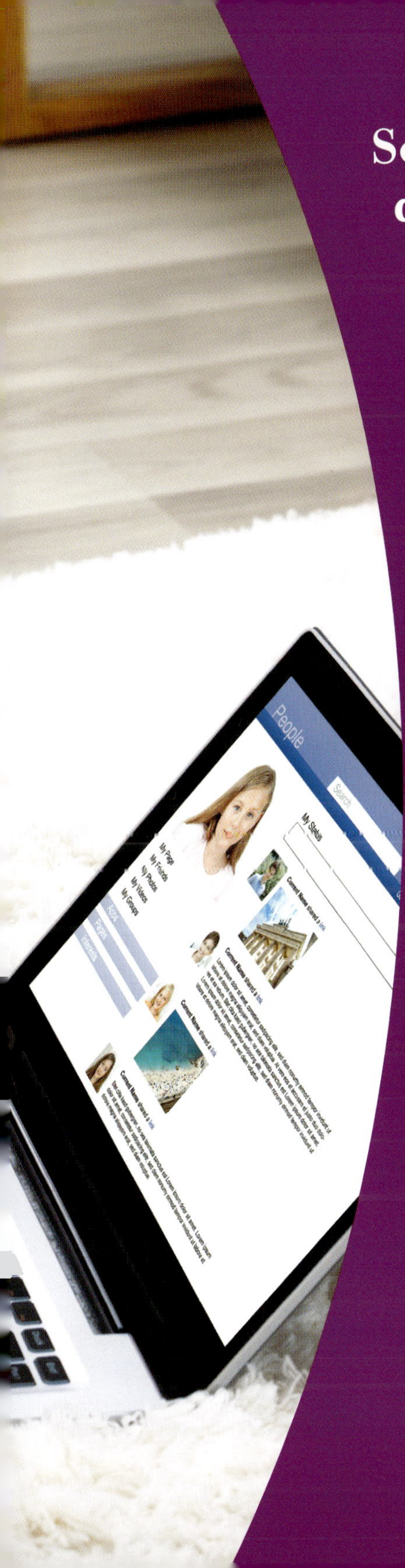

Social media has risks. But it allows us to connect in new ways. We can keep in touch with friends and family around the world. Do you use social media? If so, what sites do you use? How do you use them? If not, would you like to?

DID YOU KNOW?

Facebook started in 2004. A college student made it. It was just for students. Now it has billions of users.

ACTIVITIES & TOOLS

TRY THIS!

CREATE A SOCIAL MEDIA SITE

Some social media sites are created for a network of people interested in a topic. Design your own social media site.

What You Need:
- paper
- pencil
- crayons, markers, or colored pencils

❶ Choose a topic you are interested in. It can be a hobby, a game, a sport, an animal, or anything else. Create a name for a social media site about that topic.

❷ On the paper, design the layout for your social media site.

❸ Think about your users. Who would you want to join your social media site? Design a profile for an imaginary user.

❹ Now imagine what information users would share. Draw a post from a user.

❺ Finally, what would the feed look like? Draw it!

GLOSSARY

apps: Short for applications; computer programs that do specific tasks and are designed for mobile devices.

blogs: Regularly updated websites or web pages, typically run by an individual or small group, that are written in an informal or conversational style.

data: Information collected in a place so that something can be done with it.

feed: A collection of posts that are presented together.

hashtag: A phrase on social media that begins with a pound sign and identifies a topic.

interactive: Involving the actions or input of users, particularly related to two-way electronic communication systems.

network: A group of connected people.

packets: Small units of data that have been broken down to travel along a network.

post: To share things on social media for your followers.

profile: A description of someone's life, work, interests, or other personal information that has been posted on a social media website.

routers: Devices that guide data packets along routes over an electronic communications network, like the internet.

servers: Computers that store files that can be accessed through the internet.

upload: To send information to another computer over a network.

INDEX

apps 6
blogs 11
comment 5, 11
data 12
fake news 19
feed 11
hashtag 11
Instagram 6, 7
interests 8
message 11
network 5, 8
packets 17
photos 5, 6, 8, 14, 17
post 5, 6, 11
privacy settings 18
profile 8
routers 17
servers 12, 13, 14, 17
Snapchat 6, 7
Twitter 6, 7
upload 14
video chat 11
videos 6, 11
YouTube 6, 7

TO LEARN MORE

Finding more information is as easy as 1, 2, 3.

1. Go to www.factsurfer.com
2. Enter "howdoessocialmediawork?" into the search box.
3. Choose your book to see a list of websites.